How Does a Chocolate Maker Use Science?

By **Ruth Owen**

Design by **Alix Wood**

What is YOUR favourite food treat?

People eat chocolate in lots of different ways.

Easter eggs

Posh chocolates

Chocolate bar

Did you know that chocolate grows on trees?

Chocolate chips in cookies

Chocolate is made from seeds that grow on a cacao tree.

Cacao tree

Let's say it! "kuh-KOW"

How does a chocolate maker use science to turn beans into chocolate?

Come on little scientists, let's answer that BIG question!

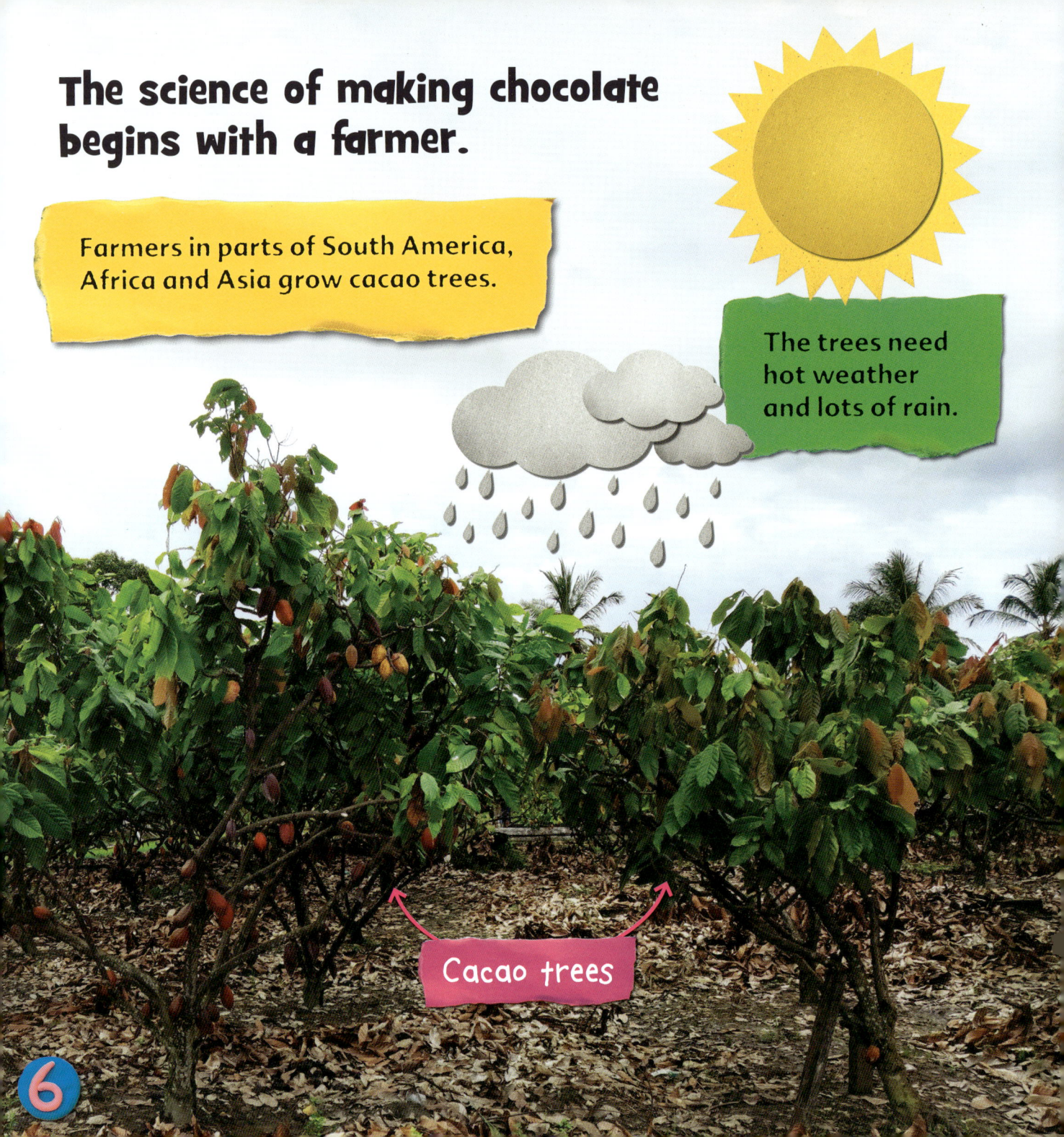

The science of making chocolate begins with a farmer.

Farmers in parts of South America, Africa and Asia grow cacao trees.

The trees need hot weather and lots of rain.

Cacao trees

Get ready for some BIG science!

A cacao tree grows tiny, tiny flowers.

Adult finger

Cacao tree flower

Cacao tree pod

Chocolate farmer

Next, mini flies called midges zoom from flower to flower carrying pollen.

The tiny flowers grow big pods filled with seeds which the farmers collect.

Without the tiny flies there would be no chocolate!

Inside each cacao pod there are up to 50 seeds.

Pod

Pulp

Seed

The white stuff is called pulp.

Chocolate makers call the seeds cacao, or cocoa, beans.

The cocoa beans and pulp are put into boxes.

Cocoa beans and pulp

Inside the box, the beans start to warm up and ferment.
- Fermenting kills germs.
- It makes the beans' shells get softer.
- The beans' taste gets better, too!

Finally, the beans are dried in hot sunshine.

Drying beans

The dried beans may travel thousands of miles on a ship to a chocolate factory.

Oven

Chocolate maker

Then the chocolate makers get to work with science and special machines!

First, the beans are roasted in an oven.

Next, another machine removes the beans' shells.

Cocoa bean shell

Soon, all that's left are tiny bits of cocoa, called cocoa nibs.

Cocoa nibs

Next, the chocolate maker puts the solid cocoa nibs into a grinding machine.

Wheel

The wheels of the machine grind and crush the nibs against a big stone at the bottom of the machine.

Crushed cocoa nibs

The grinding also causes friction which makes heat.

Try rubbing your hands together fast. They get hot because of friction.

The grinding and heat change the solid nibs into a thick, smooth liquid.

Grinding wheel

Liquid

The chocolate maker adds ingredients to the liquid.

Sugar

Milk powder

Vanilla

Dark chocolate — Less milk powder

Milk chocolate — More milk powder

Get ready for more BIG science!

Chocolate maker

Now the chocolate maker tempers the liquid chocolate by heating and then cooling it.

Hot liquid chocolate

Cold counter

Sometimes they do this by spreading the hot liquid chocolate onto a cold, stone counter.

When the chocolate's temperature is just right, it is ready.

Tempered chocolate looks shiny. It stays hard and snaps when you break it.

Tempered chocolate bar

Chocolate that has not been tempered is bendy, crumbly and dull.

Untempered chocolate bar

At the chocolate factory the liquid tempered chocolate is poured into moulds.

The liquid chocolate takes the shape of the hollow mould.

Machine pouring chocolate

Filled mould

Empty mould

The moulds are tapped on a hard surface to burst any air bubbles in the chocolate.

The chocolate goes into a big fridge to cool.

As it cools, chocolate turns solid. Then it's removed from the moulds.

Solid chocolate

The chocolate is wrapped in foil paper to keep it fresh.

foil

Some chocolate makers are called chocolatiers.

A chocolatier works in a special kitchen.

Different shapes

Let's say it! "chahk-uh-luh-TEER"

They invent new ways to eat this treat.

Chocolatiers try mixing different ingredients with chocolate to create new flavours.

Coconut

Fruit

Nuts

Spicy peppercorns

Hot chillies

Peppermint leaves

Flowers

Seaweed

Moss

Berries

They get to taste their chocolate inventions. Cool!

Roasted garlic

Marmite

Chocolatiers make paints that we can eat to decorate chocolates.

Sweet-tasting paint

They put yummy ingredients inside chocolates.

Painted chocolates

Chocolatiers use moulds to make special chocolate sculptures, or models.

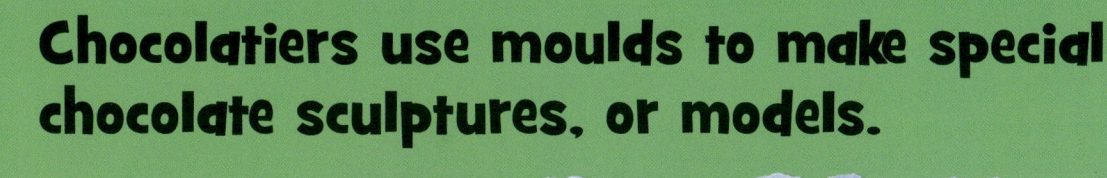

Sometimes they carve large lumps of chocolate into sculptures.

Chocolate elephant sculpture

Let's check out some BIG chocolate science again!

Crushing cocoa nibs and melting them with heat turns them from a **solid** into a **liquid**.

Solid

Liquid

When liquid chocolate cools, it becomes solid again.

And if we leave chocolate in hot sunshine, it melts and turns liquid again.

Uh-oh! That's sticky.

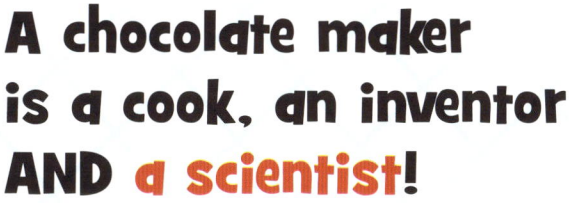

A chocolate maker is a cook, an inventor AND a scientist!

Now we know how chocolate makers use science.

Good work, little scientists!

My Science Words

ferment
To change so that a substance has a different taste.

friction
A force that creates heat when one object pushes against another.

ingredients
Different foods that can be mixed to make another type of food.

mould
A hollow, or empty, container in a special shape. When a substance in the mould turns solid, the substance takes the mould's shape.